FINANCIAL MANAGEMENT: A SIMPLE STEP

Anchit Jhamb and Swati Aggarwal

First Published in 2020

Becomeshakespeare.com
One Point Six Technologies Pvt Ltd.
119-123, 1st Floor, Building J2, B - Wing, WadalaTruck Terminal,
Wadala East, Mumbai, Maharashtra, India, 400022.
T: +91 8080226699

Wordit Art Fund helps deserving authors publish their work by
providing monetary support. To apply for funding, please visit us at
www.BecomeShakespeare.com

ISBN - 978-93-90266-05-0

DEDICATION

Affectionately dedicated this book to all the persons who want to make their first step towards Financial Management.

ACKNOWLEDGMENTS

First and Foremost we would like to thanks our parents and the almighty God for their blessings in successful completion of this book.

We would like to present deep gratitude to Becomeshakespeare.com and WORDIT ART FUND who gave us this platform to publish the book.

PREFACE

The businesses are completely dependent on finance and although business get finance the major concern is to utilize the money in the best of the manner to cover the cost and also give the good returns to the company. A business can only survive if it earns profit and there are two conditions to increase the profit the first one is to increase the sales and second option is to decrease the cost and the finance department is good at reducing the cost or it can be stated that the major purpose of the finance department is to reduce the cost by setting the trends in such a manner that the uncertainty of future is also reduced. With the passage of time financial management has emerged as different area of study and importance and many theories have also attached with it.

This book gives an easy understanding of financial management and related concepts in the simplest manner and also the students of streams related to management like BBA, B.Com, MBA, M.Com, and BBM can use this book as guidance but it should not be the only source of reliance. This book just simplifies the concept.

Contents

CHAPTER-1 INTRODUCTION TO FINANCIAL MANAGEMENT

Introduction

The term financial management is derived from two words finance and management. Where finance broadly means the study of money, investments etc and management means the set of principles relating to planning, organizing, directing and controlling to achieve the desired result. So financial management can be stated as planning, organizing, directing and controlling the sources of funds and money to achieve the desired result of increased profits and decreased cost

What is Financial Management?

The art and science of managing the money with the use of financial services and financial instruments can be termed as Finance. The business finance means to acquire and use the finance in such a manner that it meets the financial needs of the firm with the overall objectives of the firm. The financial management the process of acquiring and using the funds to achieve the profitability is termed as financial management.

What are the different types of finance?

There are majorly two types of finance available for the company. A) Private Finance and B) Public Finance

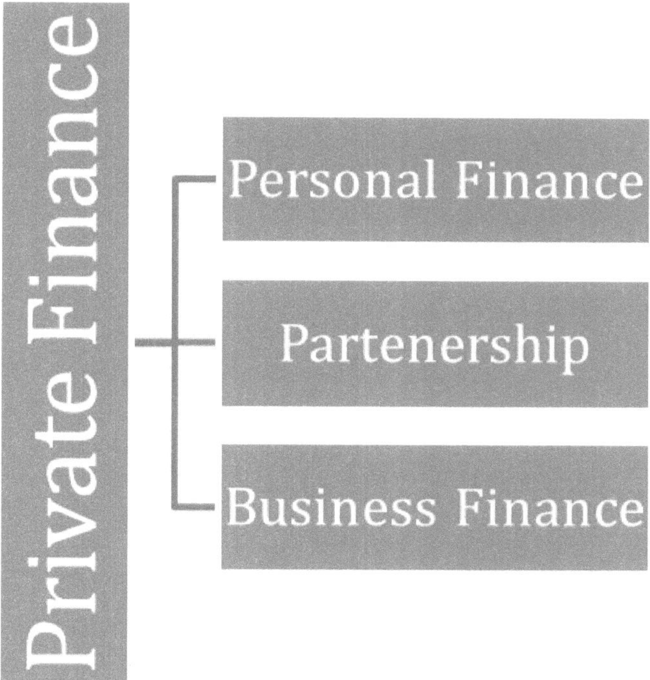

Fig-1A-Private Finance

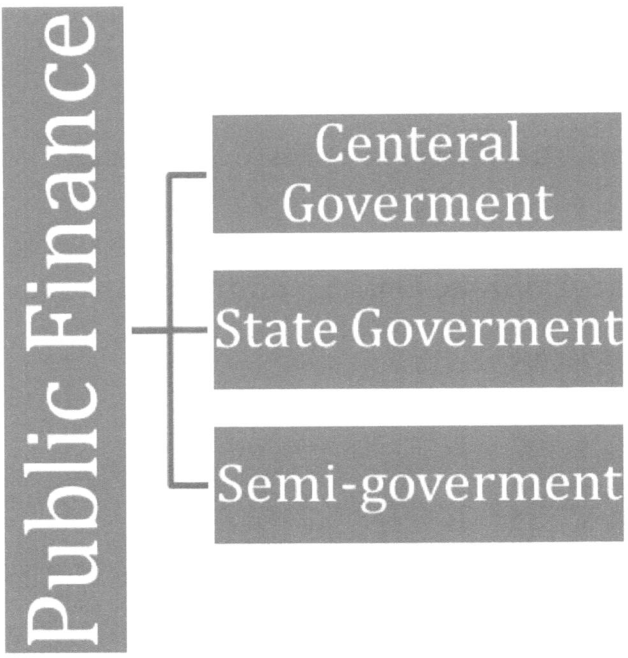

Fig-1B-Public Finance

What are the areas and need of Financial Management?

The areas and need of financial management are very wide and undisputedly it covers all the operations and functions of a company and the wide scope can also be understand from the point that the smallest unit in the economy is a household and the largest unit in the economy is a joint stock company and from largest to smallest unit there is requirement of financial management so that the risk which is created by the uncertainty of the future can be covered. And also according to the concepts of accounts there is need to plan for future expenses and losses so every unit in the economy goes through same situation and hence management is required.

Scope of Financial Management

1) **Financial Management and Economics-** Economics is the concept which works on the theory of demand and supply and one of the major decision taken under financial management is the decision of investment. So investment means earning through surplus by using some tools like equity shares, debentures etc and the same tools can be used by those companies which are having deficit of capital. And also the study of economy helps to understand the trend in demand of buyers and future conditions at national and international level and using all such facts and figures the can plan its finances.

2) **Financial Management and Mathematics-** There are many concepts in financial management which have direct relationship with mathematics and statistics like time value of money, Ratio analysis, capital structure and dividend theories these concepts of mathematics and statistics are used in financial management for the easy decision making by the finance manager.

3) **Financial Management and Human Resources-** As a human resource is selected in the organization for different operations it is a compulsory to pay that resource some consideration. And further there will be development programe, recreational activities, spiritual and motivational lectures these all things will include monetary expense and hence the Human resource department needs to have a good relations with finance department for planning and investments in human resources.

4) **Financial Management and Sales or Marketing-** Sales or Marketing is the department which a direct revenue for the company but to earn the direct revenue some kind of investments is required like hiring of sales force team which will ask for consideration and to survive in the competition advertisements will be required again investments so sales or marketing department needs to be in direct touch with finance department for the financial planning and investment.

5) **Financial Management and Accounts-** Financial Management and Accounts if taken together are the part of Management Accounts and Financial Management is only possible if the accounts are prepared and then financial manager by using accounts and financial management makes the decisions for the company.

Importance of Financial Management

1) **Financial Planning-**Financial planning is important because the future is uncertain and uncertain creates risk but risk can be positive and negative and companies do prepare for negative situations like losses, expenses and which leads to a regressive need of financial planning.

2) **Acquisition of funds-** Finance is the lifeline of business a business cannot expect to work itself for single day so either for short term or for long term or for any decision a company requires some financial backup so financial manager must find the sources to acquire with minimum cost.

3) **Proper use of Funds-** Only acquiring the funds will not do the job the proper usage is also required and usage can be in different manners but it should be fruitful for the business so that risk and cost can be covered

4) **Value of Firm-**As the business will cover the cost and will improve the profitability the name and fame of company will also improve in the market as increased and maintained profitability is one of the sources to increase the goodwill. Hence it very important to do financial management in proper manner.

What are the functions of Finance manager?

The major function of a finance manager is to control the cost of the company, improve the profitability and utilize the funds in the optimized manner and also improve and manage the capital structure of the company.

1) **Relation with other departments-** As every department and operation in the business requires financial support so it becomes the duty of finance manager to maintain good relations with all the departments and in return every department also supports finance manager for the development of department and organization.

2) **Financial Requirements-** It is the function of finance manager to analyses the future financial requirements of the company it can be any future investment or it can be a capital requirement but finance manager has to keep a close check on each and everything.

3) **Cash Management-** Liquidity means the cash in hand or the cash with the business and some liquidity has to be maintained by the business but the level of liquidity is to be defined by the finance manager and there can be many factors by considering which a finance manager can reach to this decision.

What are the objectives of Financial Management?

The are two major objectives of the business and school of thoughts is divided in both the objectives one school of thought is in favor pf Profit maximization and other school of thought is in favor of wealth maximization and both the schools have given their arguments in favor and against of each other

4) **Profit maximization-**To increase the profit of the business by reducing the overall cost of the business and second to increase the sales of the business it is considered to be the traditional approach of the business but profit is the ultimate thing which gives a soft cushion to the business to handle the risk and expenses.

Arguments in favor of Profit Maximization

a) Profit is the life line of business

b) Profit helps the business to take risks

c) Profit improves the stability of the business

d) Profit improves the liquidity of the business

e) Profit is the major source of finance

Arguments in against of Profit Maximization

a)   It makes an undue pressure on sales force

b)   It makes firm or business greedy

c)   It tends to develop immoral practices

1)   Wealth Maximization- It is the modern approach and second objective of a business. In simple words when a firm tries to increase the goodwill and share price is known as wealth maximization. This concept says it makes the working more transparent and makes the all the stakeholders to be more confident about the business.

Arguments in favor of Wealth Maximization

a)   It is superior to profit maximization

b)   It considers risk

c)   It ensures the interest of stakeholders

d)   It considers allocation of resources

Arguments in against Wealth Maximization

a)   Wealth maximization is not possible without profit maximization

b)   It is the indirect way of profit maximization

c)   The ultimate goal is to increase profitability

d)   It gives management some exclusive benefits

What are the approaches to financial Management?

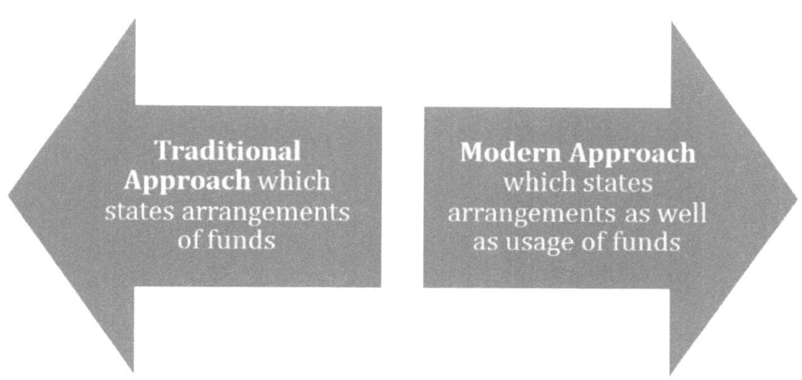

Fig-2- Approaches to Financial Management

What are the sources of finance?

Sources means the areas or the avenues from where a company can arrange for the funds and the requirement also can be for long or short period

A)   **On the basis of period**

a)   **Long term sources**

1)   Equity Shares

2)   Preference Shares

3)   Debentures

4)   Bonds

5)   Long term Loans

6)   Previous Profit and Surplus

7)   Deposits

b)   **Short term sources**

1)   Factoring

2)   Short term credit

3)   Raw material suppliers

4)   Trade credit

5)   Money Market Instruments

B)   **On the basis of Ownership**

a)   **Owned funds**

1)   Shares

2)   Retained Earnings

3)   Surplus

b) **Borrowed Funds**

1) Bonds

2) Debentures

3) Public Fund

4) Loan from banks and financial institutes

CHAPTER 2 CAPITAL STRUCTURE

Capital structure means the relationship between all the sources of finance used by the company. These sources are majorly divided into two parts A) Owned funds which can be used for long and short term B) borrowed funds again for long and short term. Capital structure also has a major impact on the value of firm or say goodwill of the firm and this has given a rise to 4 theories which are related to the capital structure. But every source has its own cost to acquire funds and it is the duty of finance manager to look out the sources and their cost and they to raise the money for the business. This analysis of raising the money by looking at cost so that minimum cost is borne by the company and maximum return can be generated from that capital is termed as optimal capital structure. The requirement of capital depends on various conditions a business is facing and depending upon the requirement of capital the finance manager tries to give modifications to the capital structure although to make the changes is tough job but cost is to be covered if changes cannot be made in capital structure then portfolio management should be appropriate.

What are the Objectives of Capital Structure?

1) Minimum Cost and

2) Maximum Return

What are the factors which Capital Structure of a company?

1) **Cash flow position-** cash flow is very important for a business if the inflow of cash is better position than outflow then dependency on the other sources of funds reduces otherwise it is vice versa and cost increases.

2) **Return on Investment-** It is a crucial factor for the company if the return on investment is greater than rate of interest then dependency on the other sources of funds reduces otherwise it is vice versa and cost increases.

3) **Tax Rate-** The finance manager will compare the interest on debt or loan (loan for easy understanding) and tax rate and in case the interest on debt or loan is lower than the tax rate then the debt or loan will be preferred.

4) **Flexibility-** Higher the debt or loan lower is the flexibility to use other funds as higher debt gives negative impression to improve the flexibility the company tries to use equity shares for raising capital.

5)   **Control and Division of Profit-** Higher the number of equity shareholders there will increase in the decision making authorities of the company and the time duration to take decision will also increase hence the control will be diluted and at the time of distributing profit in terms of dividend there will be as many shares holders demanding their share ultimately reducing the amount of dividend per share

What are the theories of Capital Structure?

The theories of capital structure have major focus on establishing a relation between capital structure and value of firm explaining the point that with the use of debt or equity or both whether it can impact the goodwill of firm the relationship can be positive or negative There are four theories related to capital structure 1) Net Income Approach (NI) 2) Net Operating Approach (NOI) 3) Traditional approach 4) Modigilani-Miller Approach

1) **Net Income Approach-** The Approach given by Durand justifies the relationship between use of debt and value of firm. This approach states that value of Firm increases with the use of debt. EBIT being constant the WACC reduces ultimately increasing the value of firm.

Value of Firm= Earnings/WACC

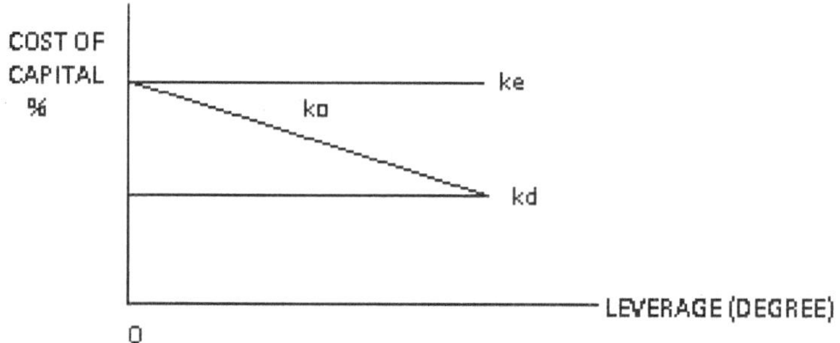

Fig-3- Net Income Approach

Assumptions of NI Approach

i) The increase in debt does not affect the risk perception of the investors

ii) Cost of debt(Kd) is lower than cost of equity(Ke)

iii) Corporate taxes does not exist

Particulars	Case-1	Case-2	Case-3
EBIT	2,50,000	2,50,000	2,50,000
(-) Interest 6%	24,000	48,000	18,000
EBT	2,30,000	2,20,000	2,35,000
KE	10%	10%	10%
Value of Equity (EBT/KE)	22,60,000	20,02,000	23,20,000
Value of Debt 6%	4,00,000	8,00,000	3,00,000
Total Value of Firm	26,60,000	28,02,000	26,20,000
WACC (EBIT/ TOTAL VALUE)*100	9.39%	8.92%	9.54%

Above three scenarios clearly identifies that with the increase in value of debt the total value of firm is increasing and WACC is decreasing which clearly gives the result that with the increase in debt the value of firm has increased. If we compare case-1 and case-2 the value of debt and value of firm has increased and if compare case-2 and case-3 and also if we compare case-1 and case-3 the value of debt has decreased with the value of firm.

2) **Net Operating Income Approach-** This Approach suggested by Durand states that there no relationship between use of debt and value of firm. This approach states that value of Firm is not effected with the use of debt. NOI approach proposes that the use of debt increases the risk of shareholders and higher cost of equity nullifies the effect of gain.

Value of firm=EBIT/KO

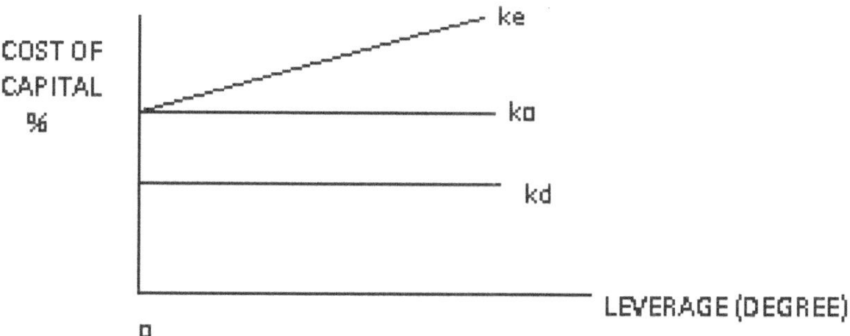

Fig-4- Net Operating Income Approach

Assumptions of NOI Approach

i)   WACC is always constant

ii)   Cost of Debt is constant

iii) Corporate taxes does not exist

Particulars	Case-1	Case-2	Case-3
EBIT	2,50,000	2,50,000	2,50,000
WACC (KO)	10%	10%	10%
Value of Firm (EBIT/ KO)	25,00,000	25,00,000	25,00,000
Value of Debt 6%	4,00,000	8,00,000	3,00,000
Value of Equity	21,00,000	17,00,000	22,00,000
Interest 6%	24,000	48,000	18,000
EBT (EBIT-Interest)	2,26,000	2,02,000	2,32,000
Cost of Equity (KE) (EBT/Interest)	9.41%	4.21%	12.88%

Above three scenarios clearly identifies that with the increase in value of debt the total value of firm remains unchanged which clearly gives the result that with the increase in debt the value of firm has remain unaffected. If we compare all the cases the value of debt has increased but the value of firm remains unchanged.

3) **Traditional Approach-**It is the mix of NI and NOI approach it is also termed as intermediate approach. This approach states that in the start the business gets the benefit of lower debt cost and after reaching a saturation point the effect gets nullified and business has to operate accordingly.

Value of Firm=Db+Eq

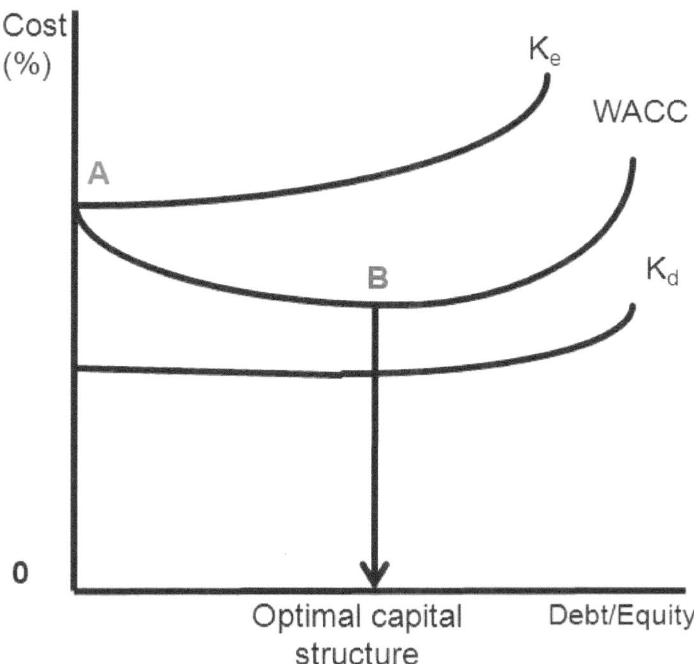

Fig-5-Traditional Approach

Assumptions to Traditional Approach

i) There are only two sources of funds employed by a firm; debt and shares.

ii) The firm pays 100% of its earning as dividend.

iii) The business risk remains constant.

iv) The investors behave rationally.

Particulars	Case-1	Case-2	Case-3
Value of Debt	----------------	4,00,000	5,00,000
Rate of Interest	----------------	12%	
Up to 4lacs	14%		
More than 4lacs EBIT	1,50,000	1,50,000	1,50,000
(-) Interest	-----------------	48,000	70,000
EBT	1,50,000	92,000	80,000
Cost of Equity (KE)	17%	18%	19%
Value of Equity (EBT/KE)	882352	5,11,111	4,21,052
Total Value of Firm	882352	9,11,111	9,21,052
WACC (EBIT/Total Value	17%	16.46%	16.28%

Above three scenarios clearly identifies that with the involvement of Debt component in the capital structure the WACC decreased and the value of firm increased and firm was also able to achieve the optimal capital structure but with the increase in debt component the value of Equity increased which will further nullify the effect of lower debt cost and hence the company has to face increased equity cost and increased liabilities.

4) **Modigilani and Miller Approach (M-M approach)-** M-M approach states that the value of firm is independent of capital structure and if the market values of identical firms are different then

arbitrage process will take place. Arbitrage Process in M-M approach states that there are two identical firms in the market one is levered firm (L) using debt and other is unlevered firm (UL) using only equity and if the unlevered firm will issue more equity shares the present shareholders will move to levered firm and the credit holders looking at the movement of more and more creditors they will move to unlevered firms as shareholders hence the balance of both the firms will remain same.

Assumptions of MM Approach

i)   There is no transaction cost

ii)   There are no corporate taxes

iii)   Investors are rational

iv)   100% payout ratio

CHAPTER 3 WORKING CAPITAL AND WORKING CAPITAL MANAGEMENT

The term working capital means the capital which is used for day to day expenses like paying utility bills, local delivery charges etc. is known as working capital. Further to make day to day expenses a business needs to have some liquidity but the liquidity depends upon many factors and every idle money in the business has some kind of cost. So a finance manager needs to plan liquidity in such a manner that it is able to cover the expenses and the company has not to bear much cost over it. So working capital means to cover day to day expenses in such a manner that liquidity is maintained at minimum cost.

What is the concept of working capital?

a)   Gross Working Capital=Sum of current assets

b)   Net Working Capital=Curren Assets-Current Liabilities

What are the types of working?

There are three types of working capital

a) **Permanent Working Capital-** When a business keeps a certain amount of liquidity with itself is known as Permanent Working Capital

b) **Temporary Working Capital-**When the amount of working capital changes with the changing business requirements. It is further divided into two parts

1) Seasonal Working Capital – There are some businesses which start their manufacturing on the basis of season like manufacturing of blankets in summer season this increases the need of working capital

2) Special Working Capital- When a business has to meet a special demand and the need of working capital arises is known as special working capital

c) **Semi-Variable working capital-** Up to a certain level the amount is kept permanent and then the amount becomes variable.

What factors affect the level of working capital in the company?

As there are many factors which affect the amount of pocket money for an individual in the same manner there are many factors which affect the amount of working capital for a company.

1) Past experience- It can be a possibility that a company must have faced some problem in past due to cash crunch and in present company has increased the amount of working capital.

2) Nature of Business- The amount of working capital dependents upon the industry to which a business belongs.

3) Business Cycle- The business has to go through many financial conditions so in case of favourable financial conditions the requirement of working capital reduces

4) Credit Policy-In case of stringent credit terms the requirement of working capital reduces

5) Production Policy-Depending upon the season of production the requirement of working capital increases and if there regular production process the requirement increases.

6) Growth and Expansion-If the company is trying to grow its business the requirement increases

What are the problems in case of wrong estimation of working capital?

In case of Overestimation of Working Capital

1) The ideal money with the business

2) Liberal credit policy

3)   Purchase of excess raw material

4)   May increase the chances of debts

5)   The increased bad debts will ultimately result in reduction of profits and reduced goodwill

In case of Underestimation of Working Capital

1)   Only cash sales and credit purchase of raw material

2)   It can give negative impact on customers

3)   Only cash sales may reduce the level of sales

4)   The reduced level of sales will directly affect the profitability

5)   Lowered profitability will negatively affect the goodwill

6)   Inadequate purchase of raw material hampering the production

Working Capital Management

Working capital management is one of the major responsibility of finance manager to idolize each and everything in such a manner that production and profitability of the firm is not affected in any manner. It is very complex task but has three major components of dependency but each one the component is again very complex.

The three components of working capital management are

1) Inventory Management

2) Cash Management

3) Receivables Management

1) **Inventory Management-**The management of stock is known as inventory management. The stock can consist of Raw material, Work in progress and finished goods to manage each of them is inventory management. The major objective to smoothen the production process and to meet the demand on time.

   There are some techniques to manage the inventory

   a) On the basis of Order quantity- Stock Level and Economic Order Quantity

   b) On the basis of classification- ABD, VED,HML analysis

   c) On the basis of record- Inventory reports and management

2) **Cash Management-** To manage the inflow and outflow of cash can be termed as Cash Management. There are some techniques to manage the inflow and outflow of cash.

   a) Slow distribution or payments

   b) Fast collection or try to receive the dues as early as possible

3) **Receivables Management**- To manage those buyers who have taken goods from the business on the credit and money is yet to be received from them.

CHAPTER 4 CAPITAL BUDGETING

To understand the term capital budgeting it is very important to understand both the terms separately. Capital means money invested by the business for some long term project and Budget means the summary of expenses a company has to bear on that particular project. So it can be assumed that the process of preparing the summary of the expenses which a company has to make in a project. And as the economics says there is scarcity of resources so a finance manager with complete responsibility has to take care that the best project is used for investment as a company is answerable to many stakeholders. And to help finance manager there are many techniques for capital budgeting. These techniques are of two types of techniques 1) traditional techniques which do not consider the time value of money and the other type 2) modern technique which considers time value of money. Before going to the techniques let us first consider the time value of money. Time value of money can be broken down into three different words Time+ Value+ Money, where time means both the present or future time, value means the purchasing power of money and money means the medium of exchange. So the time value of money means to identify the purchasing power of medium of exchange with the passage of time. If the value of money is compounded for some future period it is done through compounding techniques and if the value of money for present period is calculated it is done through discounting techniques.

Traditional Techniques

Pay Back Period- The time taken by the project to cover the cost.

Post Pay Back Period-The profit given by the project after cover the cost

Average Rate of Return-The average of the return during the complete life of the project

The decision to select or reject a project completely depend upon finance as such there is no thumb rule

Modern Techniques

Internal Rate of return- A discounting factor has to be selected by the finance manager and to select the discounting factor the present value of Inflow (P.VI) is subtracted from present value of outflow (P.VO) till the time the answer is zero.

Net Present Value- P.VI is subtracted from P.VO and then project is selected. If P.VI > P.VO projected is selected

Profitability Index- the $P.V_I$ is divided by P.VO and if the value is greater than 1 then the project is selected.

Following is one example covering all the techniques. And the discounting factor is assumed at 10%

Cost of Project-50,00,000

Life of Project- 10 years

Rate of Discount-10%

YEAR	INFLOW	DISCOUNT RATE	PRSENT VALUE
1	3,00,000	0.9091	2,72,730
2	4,00,000	0.8265	3,30,600
3	7,00,000	0.7513	5,25,910
4	30,00,000	0.6830	20,49,000
5	20,00,000	0.6209	12,41,800
6	15,00,000	0.5645	8,46,750
7	9,00,000	0.5132	4,61,880
8	10,00,000	0.4665	4,66,500
9	4,00,000	0.4241	1,69,640
10	5,00,000	0.3855	1,92,750
	1,07,00,000		65,57,560

Traditional Techniques-Decision entirely of Finance Manger as it is a single project and there is no other option

Pay Back Period= 4years and 5 months (Approx.) Post Pay Back Period= Rs 57,00,000

Average Rate of Return= Rs 10,70,000

Modern Techniques- Thumb Rule will be used for making the decision

Net Present Value=$P.V_I - P.V_O$

$$=65,57,560\text{-}50,00,000$$

$$= Rs\ 15,57,560\ (Project\ Accepted)$$

Profitability Index=$P.V_I / P.VO$

$$=65,57,560/50,00,000$$

$$=1.31\ (Project\ Accepted)$$

ABOUT THE AUTHOR

Mr. Anchit Jhamb is working as an Assistant Professor with Punjab Institute of Technology, Rajpura and has an experience of around 5 years and has written many National and International research papers in field of finance and banking. Anchit Jhamb completed his Masters in Business Administration in 2014 from School of Management Studies, Punjabi University, Patiala.

Ms. Swati Aggarwal is working as an Assistant Professor with Chandigarh University, Gharuan and has an experience of around 4 years and has authored many National and International research papers in field of finance and commerce.